Amazing Military Vehicles

ARMORED VEHICLES
IN ACTION

Kay Jackson

PowerKiDS press™

New York

To the soldiers and the Marines on patrol across the world

Published in 2009 by The Rosen Publishing Group, Inc.
29 East 21st Street, New York, NY 10010

First Edition

Editor: Nicole Pristash
Book Design: Julio Gil
Photo Researcher: Jessica Gerweck

Photo Credits: Cover, pp. 13, 14, 17, 18, 21 Courtesy of the Department of Defense; pp. 5, 6, 9, 10 © Getty Images.

Library of Congress Cataloging-in-Publication Data

Jackson, Kay, 1959–
    Armored vehicles in action / Kay Jackson. — 1st ed.
        p. cm. — (Amazing military vehicles)
    Includes index.
    ISBN 978-1-4358-2752-3 (library binding) — ISBN 978-1-4358-3162-9 (pbk.)
ISBN 978-1-4358-3168-1 (6-pack)
    1. Armored vehicles, Military. I. Title.
    UG446.5.J228 2009
    623.7'475—dc22

                                2008036663

Manufactured in the United States of America

CONTENTS

Keeping Troops Safe

Armored vehicles are used in the military every day. Some armored vehicles carry soldiers and their tools. Other armored vehicles shoot at enemies. One kind of armored vehicle is both a sea and a land vehicle. No matter how it is used, though, an armored vehicle's most important job is to keep the military's troops safe.

Today's armored vehicles are a mix of **technology**, metal, and speed. Computers and radios keep armored vehicle crews connected with each other and their commanders. Hard metals stop **bullets** and **bombs**. Powerful engines allow armored vehicles to move over uneven land and city streets.

Armored vehicles are some of the military's most important tools. These troops would not be as safe without them.

This picture shows two armored vehicles being tested by the Army in 1958. Armored vehicles from this time were built to be strong, as are the vehicles built today.

From Tractors to Technology

The U.S. military started using armored vehicles around the time of World War I. At first, an armored vehicle was just a tractor with a steel box over it. By the 1960s, however, armored vehicles had become more advanced. The M88 towed broken-down military vehicles. The M109, which is still in use today, has a large 6-inch (152 mm) gun.

Today, armored vehicles have loads of technology. They use a Global Positioning System, or GPS. A GPS is a machine that helps something find its location on a map. Now, armored vehicles are more useful than ever before.

Taking a Blast

Armored vehicles are made to withstand explosions. They are covered in armor that is 50 times harder than copper. Copper is the metal found in pennies. Many armored vehicles use composite armor. Composite armor is made up of **layers** of metal and other matter. This armor is harder than steel, and it can stop many **weapons**.

An armored vehicle's shape is also important. Some armored vehicles have a special shape that can withstand blasts better. The military is always working to find new ways to keep its troops safe from harm.

Here you can see how thick the armor is on this Bradley fighting vehicle. The armor will help keep this soldier safe from blasts.

These soldiers are on a foot patrol in Iraq. Their armored vehicle stays close by. It can bring the soldiers to safety if the patrol gets too dangerous.

On Patrol

The branches of the U.S. military that use armored vehicles are the Army and the Marines. Armored vehicles keep soldiers and marines safe as they go to the battlefield and do dangerous foot patrols.

During a foot patrol, armored vehicles go to where the enemy is fighting. The patrol's leader commands the troops to get out of the vehicles. The troops then walk around and look for hidden gunmen. The armored vehicles stay with the troops because the soldiers may need the vehicles' large guns. If the patrol becomes too dangerous, the vehicles can take the soldiers back to their base.

Moving Troops to Safety

Armored personnel carriers, or APCs, are lightly armored vehicles. APCs are not built to fight heavily in battle. Instead, an APC's job is to move troops safely. Many APCs have only one machine gun. However, different weapons can be added to an APC, like **missiles**.

The Army's M113 can do many things. It carries troops, but it can also carry supplies. An M113 can be an **ambulance** for hurt soldiers or a command post for battlefield leaders. The M113 also has metal tracks instead of wheels. The tracks help it travel over uneven roads and up steep hills.

Here these soldiers are shown putting another soldier into an M113 armored personnel carrier during a training exercise in Georgia.

Even though the Bradley fighting vehicle, shown here, weighs around 24 tons (22 t), it can travel 41 miles per hour (66 km/h).

Infantry Vehicles

Infantry soldiers use infantry vehicles. Infantry vehicles carry troops to the battlefield, as armored personnel carriers do. However, infantry vehicles can fire heavily at the enemy as well.

The Army's Stryker M1126 and Bradley fighting vehicle are infantry vehicles. These vehicles move troops easily, but they can also keep the soldiers safe with their large guns. Once on the battlefield, the crew inside a Stryker and a Bradley can send maps and messages to other crews and leaders. These infantry vehicles are built to fight in cities, too. They can easily climb over broken-down buildings.

From Sea to Land

Amphibious assault vehicles, or AAVs, are armored vehicles that can work both in the water and on land. AAVs carry marines and their tools from a ship onto shore. They use metal tracks when on land. However, in the water, the tracks are covered up. A jet **pump** pushes the AAV through the water.

On land, the Marines' AAV7A1 takes on different jobs. The AAV7A1 can travel with supply trucks or go on patrol in a city. When the AAV7A1's job on land is done, it can go into the water and go back to its ship.

In the water, these AAV7A1 vehicles can reach a speed of 8 miles per hour (13 km/h). Once on land, they can reach 45 miles per hour (72 km/h).

The Cougar, shown here, is said to be the safest armored vehicle used today. It has kept many marines and soldiers from getting badly hurt.

Cougars

The Cougar is another armored vehicle used by the military. When the Army or the Marines want to put their troops on very dangerous streets, they use the Cougar. It was made for the job.

The Cougar is the perfect vehicle for patrolling enemy streets. Guns and cameras on top of the Cougar are controlled from the inside so the crew can stay safe. The Cougar also has a bottom that is V shaped. This special shape forces explosions away from the vehicle. The Cougar is so strong that **grenades** cannot go through its strong armor or thick glass.

Armored Vehicle Crews

Each armored vehicle is run by a crew. The truck commander leads the crew. He plans patrols and looks for enemy hiding places. The driver not only drives the vehicle, but she takes care of it as well. The gunner loads and fires the vehicle's guns.

Armored vehicle crews go through different kinds of training. Armored personnel carrier and M113 crews take classes and learn to drive their vehicles. Stryker crews practice learning how to guard long lines of trucks called convoys. Amphibious assault vehicle crews train for many months in classrooms, on land, and in the water.

These soldiers are working on a Bradley fighting vehicle. Soldiers work together to take care of armored vehicles so that the vehicles run well.

New Armored Vehicles

Armored vehicles are changing as the military finds new ways to make them better. The Marines' expeditionary fighting vehicle, or EFV, is the Marines' new amphibious vehicle. On land, the EFV looks like an armored personnel carrier. However, when the EFV goes into the sea, it can change into a boat that rides easily through the water.

The U.S. military will always need armored vehicles. Tomorrow's vehicles will use new technology to make them stronger than ever before. No matter how the military changes them, though, armored vehicles will always be there to keep troops safe.

Glossary

ambulance (AM-byuh-lens) A vehicle that carries the sick or wounded to the hospital.

armored (AR-merd) Having a hard cover to keep something safe.

bombs (BOMZ) Weapons used to blow things up.

bullets (BU-lets) Things that are shot out of a gun.

grenades (greh-NAYDZ) Small bombs that are thrown by hand.

infantry (IN-fun-tree) The part of a military branch that fights on foot.

layers (LAY-erz) Thicknesses of something.

missiles (MIH-sulz) Weapons that are shot at something far away.

pump (PUMP) A machine that moves liquid or gas from one place to another.

technology (tek-NAH-luh-jee) The way people do something and the tools they use to do it.

vehicles (VEE-uh-kulz) Means of moving or carrying things.

weapons (WEH-punz) Objects or tools used to wound or kill.

Index

Web Sites

Due to the changing nature of Internet links, PowerKids Press has developed an online list of Web sites related to the subject of this book. This site is updated regularly. Please use this link to access the list:
www.powerkidslinks.com/amv/armored/